COCKNEY
RHYMING
SLANG

With thanks to the
Shadwell Blue Watch

Written by Bodmin Dark
Edited by Darwin Cannon
Illustrated by Paul Middlewick

DIRTY

COCKNEY RHYMING SLANG

Michael O'Mara Humour

Cover Photograph: James Day/Getty Images

First published in Great Britain in 2003
Michael O'Mara Books Limited
9 Lion Yard, Tremadoc Road
London, SW4 7NQ
www.mombooks.com

A CIP catalogue record for this book is available
from the British Library

ISBN 1-84317-035-3

3 5 7 9 10 8 6 4

Made and printed in Great Britain
by William Clowes, Beccles, Suffolk

Contents

7   Introduction

13   Cockney to English

107   English to Cockney

122   Over to You

Introduction

What is dirty cockney rhyming slang?

Cockney rhyming slang is a form of idiomatic speech in which a word is replaced with a phrase of two or three words which rhymes with it. Dirty cockney rhyming slang is the same thing, only much, much ruder.

Where did cockney rhyming slang come from?

The word cockney comes from cockeneyes (14th century) which means eggs that are misshapen (as if laid by a cock), and came to refer to city folk, ignorant of 'real life' (meaning rural life back then). Nowadays the definition of Cockney — and the one that most people are familiar with — is the one which originated during the 17th century. This refers to anyone born within the sound of Bow bells: the bells of St. Mary-le-Bow Church in the City of London.

It's been difficult for researchers and historians to piece together any kind of history of cockney rhyming slang, because it is largely a spoken language with very few written records. However, it is thought that rhyming slang was originally spoken in the nineteenth century by London thieves, traders and entertainers who wanted to keep secrets from strangers.

There is an element of humour and ingenuity about much rhyming slang and so it was gradually taken up by other people, originally members of the working classes. People the world over have since picked up elements of rhyming slang, and language from Australia to the United States is now peppered with cockney expressions.

How does it work?

Take a pair of associated words (e.g. Barclays Bank), where the second word rhymes with the word you intend to say (i.e. wank). In order to confuse an outsider you would use just the first word of the associated words to indicate the word you originally intended to say (as in 'Work was slow so I popped into the bogs for a quick Barclay').

About this book

Cockney rhyming slang was, and is, often used for words relating to subjects that might offend others: bodily functions, for example. But reading books and websites about cockney, you'd have thought people were ashamed of cockney's dark side.

Not us. We've poked about in the filthiest corners and dredged the deepest sewers to come up with the most disgusting phrases we could find. That means that not all of these words come from Cockneys themselves; the

11

name Cockney rhyming slang is now a loose term for the style of slang that uses the rhyming technique. So as well as traditional cockney rhyming slang we have also included more contemporary rhyming slang which has made us laugh over the last few years.

It remains to be seen if these terms will be accepted as bona fide 'Rhyming Slang' in the future, but we hope you enjoy them anyway.

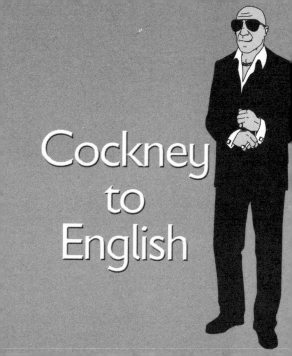

Cockney
to
English

A

Adam Ants pants

Alan Whickers knickers (Alan Whicker, British TV personality)
As in 'Don't get your Alans in a twist. I'll be home after this pint'.

Alphonse ponce; homosexual
As in 'Don't be such an Alphonse — have your dinner and come out'.

Annabel Giles piles;

haemorrhoids (Annabel Giles, British TV personality and writer)

apple tart fart
As in 'Have you dropped an apple tart or has a rat died up your Khyber pass?'

Artful Dodger todger; penis (Artful Dodger, character from Charles Dickens' novel *Oliver Twist*)
As in 'My Artful Dodger has been getting me into some dodgy scrapes

recently and he's suffering with a sore head now'.

Arthur Bliss piss (Arthur Bliss, British classical composer)
As in 'I've been drinking all day and now I'm dying for an Arthur Bliss'.

Arthur Fowler growler; fart (Arthur Fowler, British TV character from *EastEnders*)
As in 'I was on the train today and someone did an Arthur Fowler so

bad that the whole carriage emptied at the next station'.

Auld Lang Syne sixty-nine
As in 'I'm lucky if my wife gives me a hand job, let alone join me in Auld Lang Syne'.

Aunty Nelly belly
As in 'My Aunty Nelly is so big I can't see my shoes'.

B

bacon and eggs legs
As in 'Nice bacon, shame about the rat race'.

bacon bits tits
As in 'She showed me her bacon bits so I covered them with my special sauce'.

bale of hay gay
As in 'You should see how long it takes him to get ready in the

evening. He's a right bale of hay'.

ballroom blitz tits

bangers and mash slash;
urinate

Barclays Bank wank;
masturbate
*As in 'I got so bored at work today I
popped to the bogs for a Barclays
Bank three times'.*

Barry McGuigan biggun; shit

(Barry McGuigan, Northern Irish boxer)
As in 'I wouldn't go in there if I was you, I've just done a Barry'.

Barry White shite (Barry White, male soul singer)

Basil Brush thrush; vaginal infection (Basil Brush, British children's TV puppet)
As in 'I reckon she's got Basil Brush — I went down clean shaven and came up with a face

full of fluff'.

battle cruiser boozer; pub
*As in 'I'd been in the battle cruiser
since twelve o'clock and couldn't
even stand, let alone walk'.*

Belinda Carlisles piles;
haemorrhoids (Belinda Carlisle,
female US pop singer)

Ben Cartwright shite (Ben
Cartwright, American actor who
starred in TV's *Bonanza*)

berk cunt; Berkeley Hunt
As in 'I wouldn't go in that
restaurant — it's full of Berks'.

Berlin walls balls
As in 'She's always having a go at
me, banging on my Berlin Walls'.

Billy Bragg shag (Billy Bragg,
British folk rock musician)
As in 'Did you get a Billy off that
girl last night?'

bird's nest chest

As in 'She's got a nice boat race but a really tiny bird's nest'.

Black and Decker pecker; penis
As in 'Who needs sex toys when you've got a Black and Decker like mine?'

boat and oar whore
As in 'Don't listen to her — she's a lying boat and oar!'

boat race face

As in 'Nice legs, shame about the boat race'.

Bob Hope dope; marijuana (Bob Hope, US comedian, actor and entertainer)
As in 'Don't ask me — I've been smoking Bob all afternoon'.

Bob Marley charlie; cocaine (Bob Marley, Jamaican reggae musician)
As in 'Make that call and get in some more Bob Marley'.

booed and hissed pissed; drunk

Boris Becker pecker; penis
(Boris Becker, German tennis
player)
*As in 'My old Boris Becker has been
chasing skirt all over the court but
he hasn't got his balls in all year'.*

boots and socks pox; venereal
disease
*As in 'I went to Amsterdam and all I
came back with was boots and
socks'.*

bottle nerve; courage (from bottle and glass; arse. Someone who is terrified is likely to foul himself. Hence to lose your bottle means to shit yourself)

bottle of scent bent; homosexual
As in 'Get that skirt off, you great big bottle of scent'.

brace and bit shit
As in 'How much further? I'm dying for a brace'.

Brad Pitt shit (Brad Pitt, US actor)
As in 'I had a curry last night and did a Brad Pitt that would make Jennifer Aniston blush'.

Brahms and Liszt pissed; drunk
As in 'It's my birthday so I can get as Brahms as I want to'.

Brandon Block cock; penis (Brandon Block, British dance music DJ)

As in 'Don't be a Brandon Block —
let's go while you can still walk
straight'.

brandy snap slap
As in 'Shut up before I give you a
brandy snap'.

bread knife wife
As in 'I've got to get home or else
the bread knife will cut me up'.

Brenda Frickers knickers
(Brenda Fricker, Irish actress)

Brighton Pier queer; homosexual
*As in 'I wouldn't go into that bar if I
was you; it's full of Brightons'.*

Bristols tits (Bristol City; titty)
*As in 'Men have travelled from
Crawley to Carlisle for a look at her
Bristols'.*

Britney Spears beers (Britney
Spears, US pop singer)
*As in 'It's your round, so get in the
Britney Spears'.*

brown bread dead
As in 'Groucho Marx? He's been brown bread for years'.

Boutros Boutros Gali charlie; cocaine (Boutros Boutros Gali, former United Nations Secretary General)
As in 'I've had a couple of lines of Boutros and my Boris Becker is the size of a Tic Tac'.

bubble and squeak leak; urinate

bubble gum bum

bumble bee VD; venereal disease

C

camel's hump dump; shit
As in 'I couldn't wait any longer so I took a camel's hump on the back seat of the bus'.

captain's log bog; toilet
As in 'Constipation? I've been sitting

on the captain's log for an hour and nothing's happened'.

cardboard box pox; venereal disease

carving knife wife
As in 'He's got a carving knife that makes Hitler look like a saint'.

cash and carried married
As in 'Poor sod got cash and carried to a carving knife with a face like a totem'.

chalfonts piles; haemorrhoids
(Chalfont St Giles, village in
Buckinghamshire)
*As in 'I've been using cream on my
Chalfonts all week and my
underpass is still killing me'.*

Charlie Pride ride; on
horseback, in a car, etc (Charlie
Pride, African-American country
and western musician)

Charlie Ronce ponce

Charlie Smirke berk; stupid or foolish person (Charlie Smirke, British horse jockey)

cheese and crackers knackers; testicles

cheesy quaver raver
As in 'Him? He's strictly Old Skool. He's been a cheesy quaver since 1988'.

Chelsea Pier queer; odd

Chevy Chase face (Chevy Chase, American comedy actor)
As in 'She had a Chevy Chase like a bulldog licking piss off a nettle'.

chicken jalfrezi crazy
As in 'She took too many drugs when she was a teenager and she's been chicken jalfrezi ever since'.

chicken oriental mental
As in 'Drugs? You should see the rest of her family. They're all chicken oriental'.

chips and peas knees
*As in 'She must have been
desperate. She was down on her
chips before I'd got my trousers off'.*

chorus and verse arse
*As in 'She was no angel, either, the
way she worked her chorus'.*

Christopher Lee pee; urinate
(Christopher Lee, British actor)
*As in 'I got worried when he sat on
my face and asked if he could do a
Christopher'.*

Clark Kent bent; homosexual
(Clark Kent, character in
Superman)
*As in 'She's fancied him for years,
but everyone knows she's onto a
hiding; he's completely Clark Kent'.*

Clement Freud haemorrhoid
(Clement Freud, British food
writer and broadcaster)
*As in 'I've got one Clement Freud so
big that I thought my brain had
fallen out of my Khyber'.*

cobblers, cobbler's awls balls;
testicles
*As in 'Stop talking cobblers. You
wouldn't know a business opportunity
if it bit you on the arse'.*

cod and hake trouser snake;
penis
*As in 'He's got a cod big enough to
close a convent'.*

cow and horse intercourse
As in 'Six months and we still haven't

had any cow. I'm off for a pint'.

cream crackered knackered;
exhausted
*As in 'I don't have the energy. I'm
working day and night at the
moment so by the time I get home
I'm cream crackered'.*

crown jewels tools; balls
*As in 'She called him a liar and then
kicked him in the crown jewels. I
hate to see a grown man cry'.*

Cyril Sneer queer; homosexual (Cyril Sneer, character in children's animation television series *The Raccoons*)
As in 'I'm not going to the pub with you. You look like a Cyril in that pink shirt'.

D

Dame Judi Dench stench
(Dame Judi Dench, British
actress)
*As in 'A rat died under the
floorboards and the Judi is awful'.*

David Gower shower (of rain)
(David Gower, English cricketer)
*As in 'Typical! No rain for weeks and
then a David Gower just when I
want to mow the lawn'.*

dental flosser tosser
As in 'Only a complete dental would turn down the chance to go out with a woman as rich as her'.

devil and demon semen
As in 'Sleep around? She's had more of the devil inside her than the whole of the Spanish Armada'.

Doctor Dre gay (Doctor Dre, US rapper and producer)
As in 'Of course he's Doctor Dre. Have you seen his trousers?'

Donald Duck fuck
As in 'I don't give a Donald what he said. I want my money now'.

Donald Trump dump; shit
(Donald Trump, US entrepreneur)
As in 'I did a Donald Trump that was so bad, my bathroom got closed down by UN weapons inspectors'.

done a bunk spunk; semen

Dot Cotton rotten (Dot Cotton, British TV character from *EastEnders*)

Douglas Hurd 1. turd; lump of excrement 2. third; third-class university degree (Douglas, Lord Hurd, British Conservative MP) *1. As in 'I don't go to the park any more because of all the dogs leaving their Douglas Hurds all over the paths'. 2. As in 'He spent three years in the pub. It's no wonder he got a Douglas'.*

D'Oyly Carte fart (Richard D'Oyly Carte, impresario, founder of an opera company noted for its performances of the works of Gilbert and Sullivan)
As in 'On the bus yesterday, I did a D'Oyly Carte so loud that the driver went to see if he had a flat tyre'.

drum and fife wife

Duke of Argyles piles; haemorrhoids
As in 'I've been suffering with the

Duke recently. I blame it on the cold weather'.

E

Eartha Kitt shit (Eartha Kitt, US singer and actress)
As in 'I don't give an Eartha Kitt what you did last week'.

Eartha Kitts tits
As in 'She's got a pair of Earthas that would make Dolly Parton weep'.

east west breast
As in 'It's just a shame that one east west is so much bigger than the other'.

eat dim sum take it up the bum (dim sum, Chinese dumplings)
As in 'It's no surprise she's got the Duke of Argyles. Every time we go to bed she wants to eat dim sum'.

Edinburgh fringe minge; vagina
As in 'Her Edinburgh fringe is so

*overgrown that she has to tuck her
trousers into her socks'.*

Elephant & Castle arsehole
(Elephant & Castle, district in
South London; the name is said
to derive from a visit of the
Infanta of Castile)

Elizabeth Regina vagina

Emma Freuds haemorrhoids
(Emma Freud, British broadcaster
and journalist)

As in 'It takes two things to make a good doctor: grey hair and Emma Freuds. Grey hair makes you look distinguished but Emma Freuds make you look concerned'.

F

fainting fits tits

Farmer Giles piles
As in 'Why are your trousers wet?' 'My Farmers are so itchy I've been shoving ice cubes up my Khyber all day'.

feeling fine sixty-nine

fife and drum bum
As in 'You should see her in a pair of hot pants. She's got a cracking fife'.

fit and spasm orgasm
As in 'I asked my girlfriend why I can never tell when she has a fit and spasm. She said it's because I'm never home when it happens'.

Finley Quaye gay (Finley Quaye, British reggae/soul singer)

fish and shrimp pimp

flea and louse whore house
*As in 'When I was a lad I used to go
to the flea and louse every weekend.
In the end I got Pat and Mick and
my Boris Becker almost dropped off'.*

floor liner vagina

for a large fee STD

Forrest Gump dump; shit
(Forrest Gump, eponymous hero

of the US film *Forrest Gump*,
played by Tom Hanks)
*As in 'Get out of the bathroom; I'm
dying for a Forrest'.*

forty-four whore
*As in 'How was your forty-four?' 'She
wasn't too bad, but I feel a bit Pat
and Mick now'.*

four-by-four whore (four-by-
four, a length of wood)

fox and badger tadger; penis

Frankie Vaughan porn (Frankie Vaughan, British entertainer) *As in 'I've been watching so much Frankie Vaughan lately I think I'm going to go blind'.*

front and back sack

fun and frolics bollocks; testicles

G H I

G

games and sports warts
As in 'I went to the clinic the other day and it looks like I've got a bad dose of games'.

Gareth Hunt cunt (Gareth Hunt, British TV actor)
As in 'If you weren't such a Gareth I'd marry you'.

Gareth Gates masturbates (Gareth Gates, British popstar)

Gary Glitter shitter; anus
(Gary Glitter, British rock and
pop singer)
*As in 'Ask if she takes it up the
Gary'.*

general election erection
*As in 'I've got a general election
bigger than Jon Snow's
swingometer'.*

George and Zippy nippy; cold
(George and Zippy, puppets on
British children's TV)

George Martin farting (George Martin, British music producer best known for his work with The Beatles)
As in 'Stop George Martin. You're making me sick'.

Georgie Bests breasts (George Best, Manchester United and England footballer)

Gianluca Vialli charlie; cocaine (Gianlucca Vialli, Italian football manager)

ginger beer queer

glass chandelier queer;
homosexual
*As in 'It's always the same story.
Give him a stage and he starts
acting like a glass chandelier'.*

gone to bed dead

goose and duck fuck
*As in 'I don't give a goose what she
thinks; I'm going fishing'.*

Gordon Banks wanks (Gordon Banks, British footballer)

gravel and grit shit
As in 'I'm pushing cloth. I need to shovel this gravel'.

guns and bombs condoms

gypsy's kiss piss
As in 'I'm off for a gypsy's kiss, get the beers in'.

H

Hale and Pace face (Hale and Pace, British TV comedians)

Hampton, Hampton Wick prick; penis (Hampton Wick, village in Greater London)
As in 'I was driving down the road when this stupid Hampton cut me up on the inside'.

ham shank Yank; American

hand and fist pissed; drunk

Harry Monk spunk; semen
*As in 'I wouldn't go out like that;
you've got Harry in your hair'.*

Hattie Jacques the shakes
(Hattie Jacques, British comic
actress best known for her work
in the *Carry On* films)

heaven and hell smell

heavens above love

herring and kipper stripper
*As in 'I don't go to that club
anymore. All the herrings have got
saggy Bristols'.*

hit and miss piss

horse and cart fart

horse and trap the clap;
venereal disease: gonorrhoea
*As in 'I used to sleep around but
then I got a dose of the horse'.*

Howard's Way gay (*Howard's Way*, TV serial of the 1980s)

I

iron hoof poof

J

Jack and Danny fanny (Jack Torrence and his son Danny, characters in the horror film *The Shining*)
As in *'She's got a lovely Jack. I could have stayed down there all day'*.

Jack and Jill the pill (Jack and Jill, characters in British nursery rhyme)
As in *'I couldn't believe it; she told me she was on the Jack and then*

she got pregnant'.

jack in the box pox

Jack the Ripper stripper

Jackson Pollocks bollocks
(Jackson Pollock, American artist)

Jacob's Crackers knackered

jam roll arsehole
*As in 'Anyone with any sense knows
that all jazz musicians are jam rolls'.*

J. Arthur Rank wank (J. Arthur Rank, American film producer)

Jimmy Riddle piddle; urinate

Joe McBride ride; sexual intercourse (Joe McBride, American jazz musician)

Johnny Vaughan porn (Johnny Vaughan, British TV personality)

joke and farce arse

Julian Clary fairy; a male homosexual (Julian Clary, British comedian)
As in 'I knew you were a Clary when I heard you had gone for a manicure'.

K

Kate Moss toss; masturbate (Kate Moss, British supermodel)

Kerry Packered knackered (Kerry Packer, Australian entrepreneur)

kingdom come bum

King Lear queer; homosexual
(*King Lear*, play by William
Shakespeare)

Kuwaiti tanker wanker

Khyber Pass arse
*As in 'Do you take it up the
Khyber?'*

L

lame duck fuck; sexual
intercourse

lemon curd 1. turd; excrement.
2. bird; young woman
*1. As in 'I couldn't figure out why
everyone was turning their noses up
and then I realized that I'd trodden
in a lemon curd'. 2. As in 'We've got
to go to that new club. You should
see the lemon curds in there'.*

lemon tart fart

Leo Fender bender; homosexual (founder of the Fender guitar company)

Leslie Ash slash; urinate (Leslie Ash, British actress)

light and bitter shitter

Lionel Bart fart (Lionel Bart, British composer, playwright and lyricist)

As in 'It's a well-known fact that everyone likes the smell of their own Lionels'.

live gig frig; wank or fuck

lord and mastered plastered; drunk
As in 'We went to every pub in town until we were well and truly lord and mastered'.

lose or win foreskin

Lou Reed speed; amphetamines (Lou Reed, American rock musician)
As in 'I had so much Lou last Saturday I didn't sleep all week'.

lump of lard rock hard

M

Mavis Fritter shitter; anus
*As in 'If I ask you nicely will you
take it up the Mavis?'*

Magnus Pike dyke; lesbian
(Magnus Pike, British scientist and
TV presenter)
*As in 'Any woman who says no to
me has got to be a Magnus'.*

Mahatma (Gandhi) randy
(Mahatma Gandhi, Indian leader)

making a quick buck fuck

Mars and Venus penis
*As in 'I've got a Mars so big I bet it
stretches further than Uranus'.*

Max Walls balls; testicles (Max
Wall, British comedian)

Melvyn Bragg shag (Melvyn,
Lord Bragg, British TV presenter)
*As in 'Did you get a Melvyn?' 'No,
she blew me out again.' 'At least you
got something out of it then'.*

merchant banker wanker
*As in 'I had to quit my job because
the bosses were all a bunch of
merchant bankers'.*

merry old soul arsehole

metric miles piles;
haemorrhoids

Michael Miles piles;
haemorrhoids (Michael Miles,
American banjo player)
As in 'You can do what you like

down there, just watch out for my Michaels'.

Midland Bank wank

Milky Way gay

Milli Vanilli willy; penis (Milli Vanilli, music duo)

Moby Dick sick
As in 'I knew I shouldn't have eaten those cockles; I feel Moby Dick now'.

monkeys and chimps pimps

Mystic Meg third leg (Mystic Meg, British astrologer)
As in 'I wish my Mystic Meg could really see into the future; it would save me a lot of trouble the morning after'.

N

Niagara Falls balls; testicles

Nobby Stiles piles (Nobby Stiles, British footballer)
As in 'I've been sitting on a rubber ring all week and my Nobbys still hurt'.

north and south mouth

no surrenders suspenders

Nuremberg trials piles; haemorrhoids (Nuremberg trials, of the principal leaders of Nazi Germany for war crimes)

O

Oedipus Rex sex (Oedipus Rex, character in Greek mythology who kills his father and marries his mother)

ogle and leer gonorrhoea

Oliver Twist pissed (*Oliver Twist*, novel by Charles Dickens)

on the hob knob; penis

orchestra stalls balls; testicles *As in 'You'll get thrown out if you don't stop fiddling with your orchestras'.*

Orphan Annie fanny; vagina (Annie, eponymous hero of the musical and film *Annie*)

P

Pat and Mick sick (Pat and Mick, British popular music DJs)

Pat Cash slash (Pat Cash, Australian champion tennis player)

peddle and crank wank

Pedigree Chum come; orgasm (Pedigree Chum, brand of dog food)

pen and ink stink
As in 'That new aftershave you're using doesn't half pen and ink'.

Persian rugs drugs

pineapple chunk spunk; semen
As in 'She was blowing chunks'.

pogo stick dick; penis
As in 'I wouldn't mind her bouncing around on my pogo'.

polo mint bint; young girl

pony and trap crap

pork and bean queen; homosexual

Posh 'n' Becks sex (Posh 'n' Becks: Victoria Beckham, British female vocalist and David Beckham, British footballer)

R

radio rental mental

Raleigh bike dyke; lesbian

raspberry ripple cripple;
disabled person
*As in 'We lost 5-0 last week. We
were playing like a bunch of
raspberry ripples'.*

raspberry tart fart

rat race face

Ravi Shankar wanker (Ravi
Shankar, Indian musician)

Richard the Third turd (Richard the Third, British monarch)

Rick Witter shitter (Rick Witter, British pop and rock musician)

Rockford Files piles; haemorrhoids

rubber duck fuck

Rubik's Cubes pubes; pubic hair
As in 'Hairy? You could have knitted a scarf out of her Rubik's'.

ST
UV

S

Samantha Janus anus
(Samantha Janus, British actress)

Sefton Brancker wanker (Sir
Sefton Brancker, British pilot and
director of civil aviation)

Schindler's List pissed

Scotch mist pissed

Sherman tank wank

As in 'Can you leave my tea outside, Mum? I'm just having a Sherman'.

ship's anchor wanker

shoe boot prostitute

shovels and spades AIDS

sieg heils piles (sieg heil, salute used by the Nazi party in Germany in the 1930s and 1940s)

Sigourney Weaver beaver; female genitalia (Sigourney Weaver, American actress)

sir and miss syphilis

Sir Anthony Blunt cunt (Sir Anthony Blunt, British spy)

spam fritter shitter; anus
As in 'I had a vindaloo last night and my spam fritter's been killing me ever since'.

Starsky and Hutch crotch
(*Starsky and Hutch*, American
TV show)

stick of rock cock
*As in 'Let's go to the beach and you
can suck on my stick'.*

sticky buns runs
*As in 'I went to India for a month
and I had the stickys the whole time
I was there'.*

Stoke-on-Trent bent (Stoke-on-

Trent, British town in the Midlands)

Swiss banker wanker

T

Ted Ray gay (Ted Ray, American jazz musician)

Thomas More whore (Thomas More, British cardinal)

Thora Hird turd (Thora Hird, British character actress)

threes and fours whores

three card trick dick
As in 'Have you seen my three card trick? You won't be disappointed'.

three wheel trike dyke; lesbian
As in 'The problem with the women in athletics is that they may look nice but they're all three wheelers'.

thr'penny bits tits (thr'penny bits, old English coins)

Tilbury Docks pox; venereal disease (Tilbury Docks, industrial area in London's East End)

Tom and Dick sick

Tom Kite shite (Tom Kite, American pro golfer)

Tom Tank wank

Tom-Tit shit (Little Tom-Tit, character from Tit-Willow, a

song from Gilbert and Sullivan's
opera *The Mikado*)

tommy guns the runs;
diarrhoea (from the Thompson
sub-machine gun, used by US
gangsters and by the Allies
during the Second World War)
*As in 'I can't eat anything at the
moment because as soon as I do I
get the tommies'.*

Torvill and Dean queen;
homosexual (Torvill and Dean,

British figure skaters)

totem scrotum
As in 'Her sister's not much better
— she's got a face like a totem too'.

Town Halls balls; testicles

Turkish Delight shite

two-bob bit shit (two-bob bit,
old British currency)

two-bob bits tits

two-by-four whore (two-by-four, a length of wood)

U

Uncle Bob knob; penis
As in 'I pissed off my wife so she slammed my Uncle in the door'.

upper-class snob blow job

up the aisle doggy style
As in 'Before you take her up the

*aisle you'd better make sure she
takes it up the aisle'.*

V

village bike dyke; lesbian

Von Trapp crap (Family Von
Trapp, characters in the film and
musical *The Sound of Music*)

W

Wallace and Gromit vomit

Walter Mittys titties; breasts
(Walter Mitty, character from a
James Thurber short story who
spends his life daydreaming)
*As in 'I spend my whole life
dreaming about Walters'.*

wearing the smalls balls;
testicles

West End thespian lesbian

witches' cackle wedding tackle

Z

Zig and Zag shag

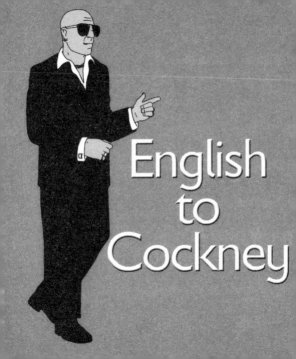

English
to
Cockney

Anus Samantha Janus

Arse Khyber Pass

Arsehole Jam Roll; Merry Old
Soul; Elephant & Castle

Balls Berlin Walls; Cobbler's
Awls; Niagara Falls; Orchestra
Stalls; Royal Albert Hall

Beaver Sigourney Weaver

Bender Leo Fender

Bent Stoke-on-Trent

Biggun Barry (McGuigan)

Bint Polo (Mint)

Bollocks Jackson Pollocks

Breast East West

Breasts Georgie Bests

Bum Kingdom Come

Charlie; cocaine Bob Marley; Gianluca Vialli; Boutros Boutros Gali

Crap Pony and Trap; Von Trapp

Crazy Chicken Jalfrezi

Cripple Raspberry Ripple

Cunt Berkshire Hunt; Berk (short for Berkshire Hunt)

Dick Three Card Trick; Pogo Stick

Dope Bob Hope

Drugs Persian Rugs

Dump Camel's Hump;
Donald Trump; Forrest Gump

Dyke Magnus Pike; Raleigh Bike;
Three Wheel Trike

Face boat race; Chevy Chase;
Hale and Pace; Rat Race

Fanny Jack and Danny

Fart D'Oyly Carte; Horse and Cart; Orson (i.e. Horse and Cart); Raspberry Tart; Apple Tart; Lionel Bart

Farting George Martin

Gay Bale of Hay; Doctor Dre; Finley Quaye; Ted Ray

Haemorrhoid Clement Freud

Haemorrhoids Emma Freuds

Knackered Cream Crackered; Kerry Packered; Jacob's Crackers

Knickers Alan Whickers

Knob Uncle Bob

Lesbian West End Thespian

Mental Chicken Oriental; Radio Rental

Minge Edinburgh Fringe

Mouth North and South

Nippy George and Zippy

Pants Adam Ants

Piddle Jimmy Riddle

Piles Nuremberg Trials; Chalfont St Giles; Farmer Giles; Nobby Stiles; Rockford Files; Sieg Heils; Annabel Giles; Duke of Argyles; Metric Miles; Michael Miles

Pill Jack and Jill

Piss Arthur Bliss; Gypsy's Kiss; Hit and Miss; Mickey (Bliss)

Pissed Brahms and Liszt; Oliver Twist; Schindler's List; Scotch Mist

Ponce Alphonse

Poof Iron Hoof

Porn Frankie Vaughan; Johnny Vaughn

Prick Hampton Wick

Pubes Rubik's Cubes

Queen Torvill & Dean

Queer Brighton Pier; King Lear;
Ginger Beer; Chelsea Pier;
Council Gritter

Randy Mahatma (Gandhi)

Raver Cheesy Quaver

Rotten Dot Cotton

Rotter Beatrix Potter

Runs Sticky Buns

Sex Posh 'n' Becks

(the) Shakes Hattie Jacques

Shag Zig and Zag; Melvyn Bragg

Shit Brace and Bit; Brad Pitt; Eartha Kitt; Tom Tit; Gravel and Grit

Shite Tom Kite; Turkish Delight;
Barry White; Ben Cartwright

Shitter Gary Glitter; Light and
Bitter; Spam Fritter; Mavis Fritter;
Rick Witter

Sick Moby Dick; Tom and Dick

Slag Toe Rag

Slash Pie & Mash; Pat Cash

Speed Lou Reed

Spunk Harry Monk; Pineapple Chunk

Stench Dame Judi (Dench)

Stink Pen and Ink

Stripper Jack the Ripper; Herring and Kipper

Suspenders No Surrenders

Thrush Basil Brush

Tits Ballroom Blitz; Eartha Kitts; Fainting Fits; Thr'penny Bits; Two-Bob Bits

Titties Bristol Cities; Walter Mitty

Tosser Dental Flosser

Turd Douglas Hurd; Richard the Third; Thora Hird

Vomit Wallace and Gromit

Wank Barclays Bank; J.Arthur

Rank; Midland Bank; Peddle and
Crank; Sherman Tank; Jodrell
Bank; Tom Tank

Wanker Kuwaiti Tanker;
Merchant Banker; Ravi Shankar;
Sefton Brancker; Swiss Banker

Wanks Gordon Banks

Whore Four-by-Four; Thomas
More

Over to You...

Awight babes, it's over to you.
Are you an expert in all things
rude, rhyming and utterly
unrepeatable? Then let us know!
Jot them down on the following
pages, then send your filthiest
examples of London's best loved
language to:

jokes@michaelomarabooks.com

124

125